Tread the Dark

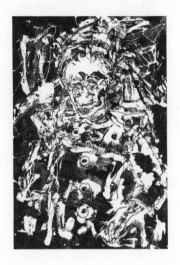

By David Ignatow

POEMS

THE GENTLE WEIGHT LIFTER

SAY PARDON

FIGURES OF THE HUMAN

EARTH HARD, SELECTED POEMS (1968)

RESCUE THE DEAD

POEMS 1934–69

THE NOTEBOOKS OF DAVID IGNATOW

SELECTED POEMS (1975)

FACING THE TREE

TREAD THE DARK

Tread the Dark

New Poems by

DAVID IGNATOW

An Atlantic Monthly Press Book

LITTLE, BROWN AND COMPANY   •   BOSTON   •   TORONTO

B

Some of the poems in this volume have been previously published in the following periodicals: *The American Poetry* (*"My writing teaches me how to die . . ."*), *The Atlantic Monthly*, *Blacksmith*, *boundary 2*, *Butt*, *Choice*, *Epoch*, *The Face of Poetry*, *Grilled Flowers*, *Harvard Magazine*, *The Hudson Review*, *Ironwood*, *Kayak*, *Lemming*, *Modern Poetry Series*, *The Nation*, *New Letters*, *Paris Review*, *Partisan Review*, *Ploughshares*, *Poetry Now*, *Quest/77*, *Rapport*, *San Marcos Review*, *Seneca Review*, *Shankpainter*, *The Sole Proprietor*, *Transatlantic Review*, *Vanderbilt Poetry Review*.

Library of Congress Cataloging in Publication Data

Ignatow, David, 1914–
   Tread the dark.

   "An Atlantic Monthly Press book."
   I. Title.
PS3517.G53T7   811'.5'4   77-28486
ISBN 0-316-41455-7

ATLANTIC–LITTLE, BROWN BOOKS
ARE PUBLISHED BY
LITTLE, BROWN AND COMPANY
IN ASSOCIATION WITH
THE ATLANTIC MONTHLY PRESS

BP

*Published simultaneously in Canada
by Little, Brown & Company (Canada) Limited*

PRINTED IN THE UNITED STATES OF AMERICA

For Stanley Kunitz

I am writing
upon the expanding wall
of the cosmos.

Contents

[viii]

Part I

1. BRIGHTNESS AS A POIGNANT LIGHT

I tread the dark and my steps are silent.
I am alone and feel a ghostly joy — wildly
free and yet I do not live absolutely
and forever, but my ghostly joy
is that I am come to light
for some reason known only to the dark,
perhaps to view itself in me.

As I tread the dark,
led by the light of my pulsating mind,
I am faithful to myself: my child.
Still, how can I be happy
to have been born only to return
to my father, the dark, to feel his power
and die?

I take comfort that I am
my father, speaking as a child
against my fatherhood. This
is the silence I hear my heart
beating in, but
not for me.

2. FROM THE OBSERVATORY

Each step is to and from an object
and does not echo in heaven
or in hell. The earth vibrates
under the heel or from impact
of a stone. Many stones fall
from outer space and earth itself
is in flight. It heads out
among the stars that are dead,
dying or afire.

3.

The seasons doubt themselves and give way
to one another. The day is doubtful of itself,
as is the night; they come, look around, slowly depart.
The sun will never be the same.
People give birth to people, flourish
and then die
and the sun is a flame of doubt
warming to our bodies.

[4]

4. WITH THE SUN'S FIRE

Are you a horror to yourself?
Do you have eyes peering at you
from within at the back of your skull
as you manage to stay calm, knowing
you are being watched by a stranger?

Be well, I am seated beside you,
planning a day's work. We are contending
with the stuff of stones and stars,
with water, air, with dirt, with food
and with the sun's fire.

5.

Examine me, I am continuous
from my first memory and have no memory
of birth. Therefore was I never born
and always have been? As told
in my breathing which is never new
or tired?

                Face in the mirror
or star hidden by the sun's rays,
you are always there but which am I
and who is the mirror or the hidden star?
Explain me as you are that I may live
in time and die
when I am dead.

6. THE TWO SELVES

I existed before my mind realized me
and when I became known to myself
it was with the affection for warmth
beside a radiator.

So you began for me
and I will whisper to your self
to give in, to surrender, to close
in remembrance, and I will give you up
and withdraw into a stone, forever
known to you.

7. THE JUGGLER

He bows and extracts from his pockets a live rabbit, tiger
cub, a rooster, a monkey, a musical instrument. Is it an
oboe? And he is ready and heaves all into the air with one
heave and quickly catches each on its way down, then
sends them up again, singly this time, one after the other.
They squawk, hiss, growl, chatter, crow. The oboe emits
music! In protest? Who can tell? It is music and that's all.
And the juggler is laughing, laughing like a clown and
nobody wonders why he uses live things.

8. SCENARIO

An old man realizes that he is seeing signs of a bodily reversion to his youth. His skin appears fresh and smooth around the thighs where it had been wrinkled and flabby; his white hair shows streaks of the original black, his sagging chin line is gone. One morning, he confronts the startling image of himself in his twenties. It frightens him and exhilarates him also, and he goes rushing to show himself to his wife who looks at him and begins to weep.

He grows younger still and leaves his wife and finds himself a young woman to live with. Life is merry again, and he grows younger still, and his new wife begins to laugh at him. He has regressed to his teens, mind and body reverting to an excitable, incoherent stage. He grows even younger, becomes a lisping child, becomes an infant, then a squalling newborn. He returns to fetus stage. He loses all sense of himself and his surroundings. He becomes an ovum. For all practical purposes, he no longer exists, but when he begins to sense himself again it's as he emerges from a wet, pulsating warm cleft with the help of a pair of forceps around his throbbing head.

9.

There's the reality: a truck passes by on the road outside my window. I have my knees crossed on the couch looking up at the trees and listening to the birds, as if I believed they had reality licked by being just birds utterly content with themselves. I could say the same for the truck but as for myself, aware of the truck, the trees and myself, my mind is restless and seeking to replace the real with its own version — also to be reckoned with.

I agree, I want the truck to pass by my house, I want the birds to sing, I want the trees to rest upon themselves, I want my knees crossed upon the couch. I want to call all this the reality. And I must settle for a question.

10.

Paint a wall
cover the weather stains
and spider webs: who's happy

You who don't exist
I make you
out of my great need
There is no prose for this
no ordered syntax
no carefully measured tread
I am falling beyond depth
into oblivion
breathing
I hear breathing
Something must be said
of nothing

I am as queer as the conception of God
I am the god and the heaven
unless I scatter myself
among the animals and furniture of earth

11.

Holes I want to creep into
and pull the cover over me
darken my mind.
I'll learn how it feels
to feel nothing.

I have a glowing heart
in an empty space.
I lie down beside it
and warm myself.

12. AN ACCOUNT IN THE PRESENT TENSE OF HOW IT ALL HAPPENED

I am about to close the refrigerator after removing a package of meat when I hear my door lock turning and a crew of men, without so much as first knocking, walk in. They stride directly over to the refrigerator, tie rope around it, hoist it upon a dolly and ride it out the door. Who are these people and why are they taking my refrigerator when there is nothing wrong with it? They are making some kind of mistake. Stop, I cry. You are in the wrong apartment. Not one turns his head to look at me or to listen. At that moment, three men, a second crew almost on the heels of the first, stride in and lift up my television set between them and walk out with it. I scream for help. I pound their shoulders but get no response, as if they were made of wood. I scream and scream, and another crew is right behind the second, this time to remove my bed. I am going to be left with nothing, nothing. I am about to get on the phone to call the police when I notice that they have cut the wires and taken the phone with them.

They remove dishes, cutlery, rugs, books, lamps; screw out the bulbs. They leave me an empty apartment and begin to tear down the apartment walls. They knock out the walls of the building itself. I flee into the street, just barely in time before they begin to attack the stairs and the elevator. Out in the street I see that it's happening to each apartment building on the block and all the tenants are milling around, with the few clothes on their backs they managed to grab and are shouting at each other in panic and wild rage. We are totally stranded; there are no police and no emergency crews in sight. The streets are beginning to resemble a bombed-out area, and we see that we will have to fend for ourselves with our bare hands. There is a park nearby and we begin to converge upon it. It has large, open spaces where we will be able to lie down and rest and perhaps make our beds there for the night with what linen and bed clothes we were able to rescue from inhuman hands. It's all over, it seems, that which gave us our comforts and pleasures. It's back to the woods and fields, and did anybody bring a knife or a gun with which to hunt a rabbit or a bird? We look at each other in the dawn of an understanding.

13. AT THE END OF THE WORLD

Emanuel puffed at his cigar as he studied the monster, twenty stories high. Emanuel, standing at its feet, each the length, breadth and height of a pyramid, looked up and down at the figure. Then as it began to bend — what a roar its movement made, like an approaching hurricane — to pick him up in its hands, each the length, breadth and bulk of a whale, Emanuel removed the cigar from his mouth and from his pocket which held a pen knife that he used for peeling apples — pulled out the knife, flipped open the blade and cut his throat.

14.

It's midnight, the house is silent.
In the distance a low musical instrument
is being played. I am alone
and it's as if the world has come to an end
on a low musical note.

15.

The sky makes no sense to me.
What is it saying? Blue? That blue is enough?
The blue of emptiness?

A small cloud trails beneath the sky
as if to make a point
about its pride in being a body,
white, welcome to the eye.

The cloud drifts out of sight.
In its absence, I will walk
beneath the sky, slowly drifting
in and out of streets and bars.

16.

I am standing on the soft, spongy surface of my brain and looking down into the space between the halves, expecting the surface to give way under my weight and hurl me down. The surface caves in suddenly and I fall. I am an object in space flying downwards, head over heels, shrieking my terror though I am falling without harm to me physically, but lost, lost without foothold, without hope of foothold. I have done this to myself, I say as I fall, and since this is what I did in all consciousness then I cannot blame myself either. It could not save me, it is no rescue, and I accept myself falling and sing out my terror like a song.

17. THE PROCESSION

It is a man held aloft on a spit
and carried over the heads of the crowd
chanting its terror and acceptance.
One of them is next.
When the corpse begins to smell
there will be a fresh one
to keep the rest remindful
of the price of peace.

18.

The trouble is that I can't occupy
the emptiness around me
while everyone looks at me
as if my desire to fill this vacuum
is some sort of madness or foolish whim.
Their eyes wide and motionless,
I fill my time walking
with hunched shoulders
in a crowd of silent faces.

19.

I wake up from a slime pit,
an unfinished man in the ages
of the flower-eating monsters:
it was the sadness of animals
who tracked their way along the given
road of their existence to its predicted end,
sprawled on their side in the snow
or in a ditch, partly eaten by another.

I missed love and tenderness on awakening
and said to myself silently,
Why am I like other creatures
when I feel myself invincible?
Am I a fool to think?

20. THE ABANDONED ANIMAL

There was an animal whose keeper had died;
the food left in the cage was plentiful,
but excrement covered the floor.
In winter he could pad upon it firmly
enough but in summer heat sank
to his joints. There was danger,
though, his body mounted on the rising waste,
the ceiling drawing close, his neck
stretched forward to give him room.

It made the poor animal whine,
to have to be crushed by his own appetite,
and at each mouthful
he could not think of the pleasure
without wanting to die.

Part II

21.

I have found what I want to do —
to kill myself quietly
I can do it slowly
in my sleep
or nourish it
in me at my work —
jealous of those
who have died
because life's needs
were endless but death
was satisfied with little.

22. THIS FALSE DESIRE

This false desire for life as I enjoy the sight of leaves turn-
ing brown, red, orange against the clear blue sky. The
leaves wave in the wind to urge me to falsehood, to make
myself a chanter of life, a bard who calls on others to live
for the glory of living. I'm tempted but I refuse, I think
death has its pleasures that I surmise from the dead who
lie very still, strictly attentive to each syllable and motion
of their death as it attends on them, stretched out like
children under the hypnotic crooning of the mother.

23.

Inside me is the peace of an egg,
round and smooth to myself,
white as a beginning.
Outside my window snow is falling
on the sagging garden shack,
so peaceful too under snow.

Peace of the snow, silence and stillness
where no figure treads.
This is a warm death
under a snow roof.
I want to live amid silence and falling snow.
I want the snow to believe me
and fall peacefully until I fall
from my place in spirals like a flake.

I hear blackbirds breaking the silence.
Keep the newspapers out of the house
and take the phone off the hook
and let the mail rot in the mailbox.
I can't take disturbance, I love the snow.
My life is happier under snow,
I nestle in my own warmth.

It will be days before another human being approaches,
the drifts are too high around the house.
Snow without fault.
I am prepared to enjoy it.

24.

Cautiously, to die cautiously
into the wind would be a way
known in a dream
and I walk into the wind
head down dreaming this wind
is the way
and I seeking to enter.

25. A RECOUNTING

I sat among the dead and heard their insides
rot and fall apart with a sigh
as it were the sound made by the dying.
In the night in the silence
amidst the cricket whirr on all sides
I heard the tearing sighs and it was like
complaining talk that it was better
to be alive, young especially, when each muscle
was firm and the body sprang.

I listened and heard more
but it was the same said in different sounds
of breaking and falling apart
and it was difficult to leave
for I felt that all being said here
I would say among the living and to say it
was to be futile and repetitious
and so I decided it was time rather to dance,
to silence their sighs by my listening
to the rhythm of my steps and I found
I had danced my way out of their midst
and upon a highway empty and stretching far off
into the distance, my blood warm, my heartbeat
fast. I danced and I danced, now a tango,
now a waltz but always a reaching out
with my legs to a deliberate passion
to meet the will I had called up face to face

to be at one with myself
to give birth to myself whole
whom I could love so that love ruled me.

I danced and the rabbits of the field came
to the edge of the road to watch
and to run across my path as a test
that I was not there to kill. They were
making little of my ecstasy and I began
to walk, throwing weary glances behind me
until I tired and sat upon a rock
at the road side and counted the ants
busying themselves around a stone
where there were holes they disappeared into
with tiny sticks and leaves between their mandibles
for building a house or a palace down below.
I had nothing to do and nowhere to go
but it was time to move to find something
to forget myself. I had danced, I had walked,
I had more yet to do before dying
when I would know that it too
was but another state of things.
I saw traffic beginning, the sun up,
and I thumbed my way back
to an angry, clamorous city.

26. DANTE'S BROTHER

There's my tiger standing in the woods. His stripes and glaring eyes go well together. He and I belong together, too. If he's hungry he'll eat me, if he can catch me. I've killed when hungry and I've ordered animals killed when others could do it better and quicker, and I have looked at the same animals alive with curiosity and made up stories about them for my amusement and to explain to myself our relationship to one another. My tiger stands perfectly still, as if he were thinking of the mystery of others too and seeking for an explanation.

27.

I hold a pair of scissors over my head and open and close the blades to cut off the air from its source. I lower the scissors to the ground and snap at the surface to punish it for its errors, such as grass, trees, flowers and fruit. I turn the scissors' point towards myself, snap the blades open and shut at my nose, my eyes, my mouth, my ears. I have to be angry at myself also who lives off earth and air.

Why is there hurt and sorrow? Scissors, cut them off from me. Scissors, whose fine steel gleams in the sunlight like a most joyful smile, why am I not like you, instead, since I must give pain? I do not want to feel it in others. I do not want to feel it in myself. I do not want to be a man, cutting through grass and flesh in the sunlight.

28.

I am dreaming of the funeral of the world, watching it go by carried in an urn, reduced to ashes, and followed by a horde of mourners, a million abreast, across the broadest lands and all chanting together, We are dead, we have killed ourselves. We are beyond rescue. What you see is not us but your thoughts of us, and I who am observing in terror of it being true hope not to have to wake up, so that I may let myself discount it as a dream.

29. APOCRYPHA

People came to watch him
chew on steak or pear
and spit out the pulp.
He sat cross legged
or moved about silently,
shaking hands mildly
or patting a shoulder,
speaking always in low, pleasant tones.

What was to be made of this man
who did not eat, drink or defecate
in the world. He seemed
to want only to taste its fruits
and let them go, happy
that the world had so many
wonderful flavors. It was this that
irritated observers, and many
hated him, after secretly trying
his way, and starving, shrunk
to skin and bones. It proved
to them he was not human,
and so he died.

30. THE SUICIDE

I find I have opened a vein in warm water and watch with curiosity dark red flow over the surface in long wavery patterns beautiful to see. Soon the surface will be covered and already I am drowsy, wondering how to stop the flow. My arms are too weak to raise me from the tub and if I do not do something quickly I'm going to die.

I am not curious about death, its absolute silence. I shall not be able to appreciate the beautiful wavery patterns of my blood. Now I cannot even call for help. I resign myself to having done what I did so that I may die at peace with myself, peace at last as I have not had in life, pushing myself to be other than what I was. I was a man who loved his ease and his thoughts and who wished only to stare out the window, but knowing that he had to act to be acknowledged as a man, I have acted.

31. THE DEAD SEA

It is so still that tracks have been laid
on piles driven into the bottom; and now
people ride their trains, occasionally curious
as to the origin of this sudden collapse
of the sea, but take it as a good omen
for traveling and communication. No wild winds,
no tall waves that ships especially designed for
had learned to climb, trained seamen
in command: a universe of dread abandoned.

One man states having patted the snout
of the once fierce meat-eating shark;
it exposed its teeth in a grin,
and now cameras daily ride the trains;
and it has been rumored the water turns
to glass when eyes are averted — an amazement
to travelers who now move quickly
and peacefully to and from business.
One man, it has been verified, dived off
the first trestle crossing and has not come up
since, in company of the fish,
swimming among them. Reading about it,
the people shuddered.

32. THEME AND VARIATIONS

How do you get to scream the world is good
and we have only to lose ourselves in its goodness?
Ask me in return and together we'll question
each man, woman and child we meet,
and won't it be the Lord's Prayer
if we all get up on our feet and shout
out the question rhythmically
because it is a passion
to know.

·

You sit drinking milk
knowing your faults,
milk drinking
your last gesture
to childhood.

·

Look at my smooth face
cover my failings.
I smile, I add
to the picture of health.

·

You strike me
and I'll strike you
and when we are through
beating each other
nearly dead, about to die,
we will be close
to an understanding of ourselves

as wanting to die
in the quickest, most efficient way
without sacrificing pleasure
as a principle of life.

•

There's love in me like an egg hardened.
What do you think would have emerged
if it had been kept warm
and allowed to hatch?

•

I am an affectionate man,
I love the differences
that compose me.

33.

I am going to where nobody else can be heard
talking, so wide and lonely a place
that when I talk it will be to myself,
puzzled by it, judging a stranger,
pronouncing good or evil because it is necessary
to know which for my own, the speaker's,
commitment to his place. It will echo
him, will make him listen to himself,
to suffer the fool gladly.
I am going off into the hardness
we reserve for ourselves.

34. SUICIDE IN TWO VOICES

Shit on this world.
What did I say?
Shit on this world.
I don't have any compliments for it either. I
    couldn't care less.
Oh fuck you too for being shocked.
I'm not shocked.
Even Beethoven sounds genteel and romantic,
    crying to his soul.
I'm giving him the door. I'm not being whimsical.
Get the hell out of here.
I'm angry.
I'm a god damn human being.
Hey, man, do you like what I'm doing here?
Who cares if you don't, you human being.
Go shoot more of your own kind.
What are you hanging around here for,
    listening to me shoot off my mouth.
Go, go to hell.
I shit on all of you, the living and the dead.
Sue me.
You rapist pig.
You're only happy when you kill.
Well, so I am, killing you off with this. And
    now I'm all alone,
as far as I'm concerned, and I'll put this
    poem through my skull.

35.

I say hello to the grass, it stays silent. I say hello to the ground, hello to the trees. I say hello to myself — "But you I know, I need an answer from the others."

I should plant trees and grass in my mind, pour earth into my thinking. It works, I grow silent, too. I do not know my life from theirs.

36. DEATH OF A LAWN MOWER

It died in its sleep,
dreaming of grass,
its knives silent and still,
dreaming too, its handle bars
a stern, abbreviated cross
in tall weeds. Where is he
whom it served so well?
Its work has come to nothing,
the dead keep to themselves.

37. IS THERE A VALUE TO LIFE?

Four squares, two below, two placed on top, combine to form a new and larger square. A fifth makes for a problem. It either should be removed or broken up and distributed among the others or placed as a sort of cap or peak. It could be kept moving over the surface of the four squares and stopped only at those particular parts that seem congruent with it at that moment. It could be made to wander as a kind of roving observer or explorer over every side. It could be placed at the very center of these four squares spread apart, with an edge of each resting on an edge of the centered fifth square.

Finding these suggestions unsatisfactory, why not mold all five into a ball? But that would eliminate their identity. Then suppose we mark off on the surface of this ball an area which each theoretically occupies, labeling each area One, Two, Three, Four and Five respectively. Would that be fair? In a way, yes. Still, none would remain intact in its original shape and so the problem of identity would not be solved.

Well, is identity necessary? I'm relieved to think about that openly.

38. CANNIBALS

I bite off a strip of my own flesh
hanging from a red wound
and it tastes sour. God,
I am startled; no, shocked —
I must admit, and I think
of cannibals. Why would they
want to eat people at all,
once tasting their flesh?
I spit out my piece,
rejecting my body, my life,
feeling guilty and ashamed.

39. THE SPORTSMAN

Shutting out the cries of the dying and hungry, the imprisoned and the tortured, beginning life all over again in innocence under the sun in sweat and energy for myself as a person, to celebrate myself once again and for always, now that I know the worst, that I must die in any case, I am on the handball court, shouting and playing my way through the miseries of others, making myself a figure of the beautiful life.

Players join me in the game and when we smile at each other we are sharing the secret, and when one of us wins, both panting from exertion, the winner is courteous and deferential so that the loser may reconcile himself in good spirits.

40. SOUTH BRONX

Where am I in all this? Under a heap of rubble some-where in the middle, awaiting the nose of the rat to sniff me out and to think a moment of my human smell. The rat will find it hard to understand, back off, bare its teeth, turn tail and run. But I am nothing at all. I am refuse. I am a junked body. I cannot be repaired. I have damaged irre-placeable parts, eyes that refuse to see any longer, turned in on themselves, arms that stick to my sides, unable and un-willing to move, out of a lack of anything for them to do, legs stiff and straight out before me, never having had anywhere to go, never put to use to walk the world. My stomach is shrunken and beyond food because what I was served as food never really fed me. But I could be useful. I am garbage like any battered open can or empty milk carton. I want at least to be found useful by the rat to re-gain pride in myself before I moulder into insensibility. If he hates and fears me then it's because it was my species that hunted him at one time and forced him to eat garbage in secret humiliation. He is confusing me with my own kind — if only he would understand, and I could help by becoming unrecognizable, a pulp of flesh.

41.

Who could have believed it? This is hell and I am looking out upon trees and grass. The air is calm; it's the beginning of Spring and soon the leaves will sprout and give us a green hell and a warm sun and a lake to swim in to cool us off, and then to dress and dine towards an evening film of hell as others live it which surely we will enjoy for its art and conviction and in private admit to ourselves its truth but that it should be lived since living has no other form for us. Rise up from your seats, ladies and gentlemen, and turn in for bed, locking your bodies together to affirm yourselves.

42. THE FOREST WARDEN

I notice the earth is not shaken by this fire
though it lies blackened and silent. I notice too
that the air is floating seed pods down onto the ground
beneath the ash from which they should emerge
in time as tiny shoots. Nothing would spring from me.

Another man would have to take my place
at the table and walk through the dead forest
searching for life, if he were curious and full of pity.
I would die neutrally.

I was happy for awhile
which said something for the usefulness in being born.
I have been sad much longer and in doubt
which also speaks of a purpose, hidden from me or lost.
I say let this fire burn and let this man that I am
die in the fire or try to save himself.
Whatever I do is a fire.

43. THE ONLY ONE I KNOW

The leaves turn and twist in the wind
as if quarreling with one another
and with themselves. Several fly off
to their death upon the ground
where they are carried along
like torn dollar bills.
The wind has enclosed my head in its pressure.
How nice it would be
to tumble along the ground,
all my living hopes for my own kind
disproven anyway.

We move around each other,
we are not harmful. We are events,
right as volcanoes.

Black trees, the irreducible pain
of the missing happiness, forgetfulness gone,
finish of pleasure. Buildings stand,
raised by an effort, himself needing his own will
to remain upright. "Unknown cause, existence of my body,
I go with you only because I feel you and I are one,
the only one I know."

44.

I am plastering myself into the wall of an apartment house. I want to be secure against any further wandering or abuse of myself. As part of the wall of a new apartment house, I can rest assured of serving the cause of shelter and other humane considerations. It will be a pleasure to listen to the sounds of music and talk piercing the wall on a pleasant night or day. I also can listen in on some heavy problems and, of course, those intimate pleasures reserved only for couples in the privacy of their bedrooms. Am a plastering myself into the wall for that purpose, really? Then I will live a long and exciting life, simply by standing upright.

Now I wonder whether I should invite a companion to stay with me, a woman I could trust who would enjoy my pleasures and approve. Together we could listen in on others while ourselves remain secreted. I hurry the job of plastering myself in, not waiting to call or write to the woman of my choice. She will know easily enough, I be-lieve, what I want of her when she hears what I have done and will simply do the same, a few bricks above or below me. It really doesn't matter. I'm indifferent as to where, just so long as we stand together in the same wall.

45. THE LIFE THEY LEAD

I wonder whether two trees standing side by side really need each other. How then did they spring up so close together? Look how their branches touch and sway in each other's path. Notice how at the very top, though, they keep the space beween them clear, which is to say that each still does its thinking but there is the sun that warms them together.

Do their roots entangle down there? Do they compete for nourishment in that fixed space they have to share between them, and if so, is it reflected in their stance towards one another, both standing straight and tall, touching only with their branches. Neither tree leans towards or away from the other. It could be a social device to keep decorum between them in public. Perhaps their culture requires it and perhaps also this touching of branches to further deceive their friends and associates as to the relationship between them — while what goes on beneath the surface is dreadful, indeed, roots gnarled and twisted or cut off from their source by the other and shrunken into lifelessness, with new roots flung out desperately in a direction from the entanglement, seeking their own private, independent sources. As these two trees stand together, they present to the eye a picture of benign harmony, and that may be so, with both dedicated to the life they lead.

46.

Smash myself against a wall
to feel how deeply I love life
in protest at the silence
in routine work to keep a house.
Silent house, its anguish stilled
in bed under covers in the night
of no history and no memory.
Night without appetite,
zero night, ringing ears listening
to silence of no future. Night
of fixation on death, seeking it
like sex, pursuing it awake
and in dreams and token deeds
to bring it on — and then the laughter
of a pepsi cola kid outside
who howls his adolescence,
smashes the bottle against the curb.
I laugh. He is in my company,
with the first smashed bottle.

47. A MEDITATION

There's no gun powder for my gun
I want to shoot a lion
I want to put on a lion's skin
I want to be a man
I want to kill myself bravely
as a lion   I want to be joyous
I want to live   I want love
I want myself

I want to be born again
I want everything
I do not want sadness
I do not want myself
I do not want pleasure
I do not want happiness
I want sacrifice
I want to sacrifice myself
I want to be God's confidant and right hand
I want mercy and pity and love and gentleness
and warmth and honor and blessing and victory
over my sadness
I'm a lion
with a gentle face
and I can be killed with ease

I am you, best friend
Why am I so sad

I am filled with promise
I exude confidence
I am a grave
I want to be obvious about it
filled with its own dirt
and nothing else
There's nothing you can tell me
or do that could move me
I am waiting at the end of the world

I am neither happy nor unhappy
I am somebody you know
We never met

48.

I placed myself inside an iron cage and threw away the key to experience being trapped, but now someone appears and thinks this actually is what I want. I have been standing silently, gripping the bars through morning, noon and night, as he notices, on his way to and from house or work, and his curiosity is no longer aroused. I can't ask him to find the key because he will then realize that I am imprisoned unwillingly and become suspicious and call up the police. I am in a vulnerable position, of my own doing.

Well, I will live out this self entrapment as best I can, with dignity and smiles to all who come upon me so that they think I am perfectly happy in my role. Oh, I can expect admiration and applause, interviews and the public press. I shall have to affirm my willingness to be self entrapped and learn how to enjoy the wonder it will arouse among my witnesses.

49. AT THE MUSEUM

This wax figure against a wall moving
arms, legs, head at a push of a button
in its palm and with label reading, Official Version,
pinned to a lapel, resembled me.
I looked around, frightened
and began to walk off as casually as I could,
turning my face from those coming in
to push the button. It talked.
I heard my voice saying I was well
and thank you and how are you
and good to see you and let's meet again —
everything I'd say in everyday exchange
in and out of office hours —
this very same figure inviting a colleague
home for dinner, with wife waiting
graciously at the door, and this invited person —
but it was another wax figure;
I saw its eyes staring ahead
until my form reached over and pressed
the button in the guest's palm.
I ran. I am home.
I waste time. I lie around.
I drink sodas, I think a lot.
I shall not leave this house again.
I have been made useless,
I can be thrown away.

50. THE QUESTION

I dream I am flying above the city
on the strength of my two outflung arms
and looking down upon the streets
where people are like so many
bacteria moving about upon a slide.
I am alone up here, with no one
to contradict me, free of the noise,
tumult and violence of the living.
Here is my true residence,
and if I say the people are bacteria
who will deny it? I declare
in my circumstances that the people
are what I say they are. The only
question now is whether I can
keep flying.

51.

I'm afraid to open the door,
something will come at me,
I'll scream and want to die
quickly in its grasp.

I'm afraid to open the door
to see myself behind it
with mouth crushed open
trying to stand up straight.

I'm afraid to open the door
to what I've been evading,
my guilt at others loving me,
devious and a liar, myself
in a coat of shit behind the door.

But what if I am standing there
behind it smiling at my fears,
my arms embracing me?
I'm afraid to open the door.

I sink back upon the ground, expecting to die. A voice speaks out of my ear, You are not going to die, you are being changed into a zebra. You will have black and white stripes up and down your back and you will love people as you do not now. That is why you will be changed into a zebra that people will tame and exhibit in a zoo. You will be a favorite among children and you will love the children in return whom you do not love now. Zoo keepers will make a pet of you because of your round, sad eyes and musical bray, and you will love your keeper as you do not now. All is well, then, I tell myself silently, listening to the voice in my ear speak to me of my future. And what will happen to you, voice in my ear, I ask silently, and the answer comes at once: I will be your gentle, musical bray that will help you as a zebra all your days. I will mediate between the world and you, and I will learn to love you as a zebra whom I did not love as a human being.

Part III

53.

I'm alone and none of my furniture
comes forward to comfort me: the desk
stands silent against the wall; the bookcase
will not move from its corner; the filing
cabinet is fixed in its place. I am
alone among the world's goods such as they are,
but who will get them to speak to me
or to act in their own behalf, dumb things
that they are, with no sense of themselves
or of others, and so I grieve,
my loneliness filled with their presence:
I exist.

54. THE VASE

See how tall and straight I stand
with blossoms above me. Could anything
be more beautiful than I who am nothing
but an enclosure upon emptiness?

If trees which have the best life of all,
belonging in one place and never moving
yet always renewing themselves,
if they don't complain when they must die
why should I, who have a far more restless
existence? I should be glad
to die into some permanent place
in the earth, and because I am not glad
and seek after the life of the trees,
I remain fixed in my own unhappiness
which is a place I cannot leave
wherever I go on earth in search
of peace, and since I have a kind of permanence
in which I should content myself
I am identified with trees.

56. THE METAMORPHOSIS

Bumping against rock in the dark,
he becomes the rock, stiffening in pain.
It fades and he becomes the lightness
and relief. He moves
and becomes the movement.
A rock is in his path once more;
he falls to his knees
in awe of his past self.

His knees make him a suppliant
of his changes. He seeks to know
and becomes a form of the curious.
He touches himself at all points
and becomes his hands.
They touch stone,
a change he remembers,
and he becomes the remembrance
and moves nimbly in the dark
from rock to rock.

57. THE EXPLORER

I have this mountain to climb
and no one to stop me,
this dangerous mountain
of glaciers and gaunt cliffs,
and I will climb it
for the sake of the living.
Climb, then, they call out,
and die. Climb, then, I answer,
softly, and live. I am
about to begin.

I am reaching for possession.
Climb, then, they whisper, and live.
Climb, then, I reply strongly,
and die.

My joy is in the trees and grass,
the rocks and glacial face
of the mountain. My joy is skyward,
my life is the opening of heaven.
I have placed my foot on the mountain
that I have discovered is my own.

58. IN MY DREAM

I've made an order for myself and it is through its tightly fitted parts that the child returns. He keeps sneaking back and running gleefully from one statue to the next, smearing each with crayons and muddy fingers. As I chase after him to drive him out, he hides behind my great, stone monoliths. He can dash from statue to statue before I even start to run. He holds in his hand a doll that squeaks when he squeezes it. He fondles it and croons to it that it belongs to him. It's all his; he will let no one touch it, and he sticks out his tongue at me as I reach to grab the doll from him so that he might grow up and become as I am, stolid, stoic, enduring.

He escapes me with his squeaking doll, and I begin to see the humor of it. I'm sorry for him trying to return after I excluded him. He must see something to want to come back, so now I let him play around with my most valued art: the statue of respectability, that of congeniality, that of cooperativeness, of the concerned citizen and many, many others that I wander among in admiration of my sculptural talent, living among the evidence, eating my bread at their feet and making my bed against the gallery wall, becoming in sleep the figure of peacefulness and fulfillment. The child tickles me on the nose as I sleep, and I rub my nose sleepily, knowing dimly in the back of my mind that it is he teasing me. I don't mind; he loves me with all my self satisfactions. He needs me, apparently. He needs someone to play with; he will play with me in these circumstances, and I tell myself, Why not, he gives me affection. All my statues are silent. When I speak he mimics me. When I raise my hand to begin a new work he mocks me with his doll that he pretends to shape with his finger and with solemn face. I shall be making new statues of all kinds: to goodness, to contentment, to pleasure, to happiness and so on but each now will have the child's influence, just that touch of humor by which I will be separated from the thing itself, and the child and I will enjoy ourselves together, and the old silence within me that made me uncomfortable and drove me to forget myself in work will have vanished in laughter between us.

Did you know that hair is flying around in the universe? Hair trimmed from beards in barber shops, from mustaches at the mirror, from underarms, from crotches, legs and chests — human hair. It all gets dumped into a fill-in space and then the wind gets at it and sails it back into the cities and towns and villages, right through your open windows during summer and even during winter down your chimney. Hair, brown, black, red, white, grey and yellow. They get all mixed up and you find them on your pullover sweater and wonder who did you come up against with yellow hair which you happen to like and you dream of its actually having happened that you were in touch with a person with yellow hair.

That's not the whole of it. Think of walking through the street on a windy day or even on a calm, balmy day. The hair is floating all around you and you are walking through, perhaps an invisible or fine mist of cut hairs. Black, brown, red that you would not have cared to touch in a million years because you associate them with certain kinds of faces and behavior but there are the hairs of these people touching and clinging to you, as if trying to tell you that hair is everywhere and everybody has it and that it's hopeless to try to pick black or brown or red off your sleeves but not yellow hair.

It would be an act of insanity. You need to pick them all off or none and let yourself be covered by them all, like a new kind of fur coat or perhaps a new hairy skin to protect you from the weather. Hair of all colors. What a pretty sight that would make, wouldn't it, and you would have a coat of many colors, and I bet you would be proud of it, especially if you saw everyone else wearing a coat of many colors. How about that? Because people cut their hair and let it fly out over the world where they land on everyone and everyone is sharing in the coat of many colors.

60.
To Charles Reznikoff

I think I am being swirled like a leaf
and I think there is wisdom
in letting myself go
and looking with a careful eye
for a landing place or a calm shoal
of wind. I say this because
I do not think it is a wind
that can be resisted
without being torn apart
and I am not mistaken;
this is the faith
I must have,
not to think life and death
synonymous.

61. THE PLEASURE

When I watch myself
grow old and grey,
I am authentic, I say.
I belong with the others.

Body, listen to me:
we don't have long to live
together but when you have
crumbled into dust
stir yourselves
when the wind blows
and fly.

62.

Standing by the sea I hear myself
being called to die in the sun's gleam
in splashing tide and bird call
sounding for fish.
All my ten fingers dig the sand.

Ocean's love is in me probing.
I am proud to be asked.
My death must count for something.
I live to find out.

63.

I touch the flesh around the skeleton
letting my hand follow its curves.
I grasp it firmly in places,
caress it where I should, probe
with my fingers where I may.
I'm delighted by the feel of flesh
and its contours, its depths,
its wetness, warmth, hair, shades
of white, brown, olive. I breathe in
its subtle exhalations. I am thankful
for the skeleton that supports my body.

64.

I am alone and I feel my important thoughts
turn against me. I grow weak, fall down
and bury my face in my arms.
I shall soon pass, I cry. Release me.

And I have died and stand up, freed,
for the earth is all I know now,
its trees and grass, and I will walk
among them because they do not rise against me.

I will live to praise the earth
with my presence and give it to my children
as my gift.

65.

In this dream I do not exist. This I know since it is my dream. How have I come to that conclusion when it is I who dream it? No one else thinks I do not exist but no one has enquired because no one knows I am dreaming. Therefore, since to myself I do not exist, it is true simply because I say so. This, then, is the problem: when I cease to dream will I exist or not exist?

I would like to become nothing for the pleasure of the great leap beyond being that becoming nothing alone can achieve. I can become nothing because I am something and I am something because it can lead to nothing. Can I ask of my life more than that it bring me to its transcendence, that I should be in search of it, as the work of being itself?

My dream, then, of not existing is my being telling me where I must go and what I must welcome as the rounding out of my completeness. I say this in the best of health and in expectation of a long life.

66.

I look the sun in the eye:
Whom do you love, I ask.
The sun never replies
but I know the truth:
it loves itself,
so there: living together
in the same universe
and getting along.

67. FOR STEPHEN MOONEY: 1913–71

I saw a shadow on the wall
weeping
spreading itself
The wall darkened
and the one brightness
was the light overhead
I saw no body of the shadow
darkness was its body
needing no man no woman
and there was darkness
comforting
relieving me of their darkness

And who were the parents of darkness
I suspected the light that spread itself
absorbing
pregnant with darkness
and this is what I know
until the born dark
absorbing light
gives birth to light

68. IN THE DARK

I'm seated beside my phone
waiting for a call
that will tell me everything
is settled; live as you've always
wanted to, and I keep waiting.
Only nighttime brings me
to lie down, with the phone still
beside me, waiting for it
to ring in the dark.

69.

Praise the worker bees that can sting
on provocation. Praise their wanting
to be left alone in their own lives.
Praise their dedication to community
and willingness to die with the sting.

And praise the sting on my left arm.
I run as fast as I can to the drug store
for a pain reliever, already dizzy
from the effects of the sting.
And praise the pain reliever,
it goes together with the sting.

70.

Conceal yourself behind the rock
and call out his name and offer help,
your hand thrust out so that you
do not see the face or the shaking hand
and can lean back
against this rock to turn your face
up to the sun, you in your body,
and in your face and in your pleasure
and in this love. But turn to give of yourself
from behind this rock what you can give,
as the sun gives and turns away
in the evening to keep itself.

71.

At night I think I will meet the one
overwhelming revelation that will set me
straight as from my youth, cost what it will,
and I make ready to grapple with it,
when peace, peace comes, though I am awed
by its night and strangeness.

It was true the earth potentially was a bomb
needing man's ingenuity to set it off
and that men worked on that prospect
in their studies and that every.man
in the street was made of nerves
needing a slight jar of an elbow
to ignite him and that with the expected
death of our globe we had abandoned
our manners: we saw men's throats
cut in offices and in the streets.
Still, we had to think first
of our comfort and of our families
and the few beauties we clung to
for relief — like the bunched daisies
or the look of poplars in the rain
in a distant field. We thought they were
tall men who had come down to visit
and wore tall peaked hats against the sun.
The daisies spelled sunshine in peace,
our families of a Sunday in the congregations
of the living. Our money would suffice
until immolation and our homes stand until —
and our pleasures the same. It was worth
believing in these few things
that padded out the time
until we thought, starting,
But we are alive!

73.

I live admiring the sky
and the mountains and loving
the day and the night, so glad
they are with me, my eyes open,
my nostrils breathing air,
my feet beside the lake,
the sea sound of my heart's beating
at anchor up and down
in the slow swell,
my life oceanic
reaching into the distance.

I am brother to the tree,
runner with the rabbit
who twitches his ears in the silence.
I cannot figure my own cost,
not in money, no more than I can count
the wind that wraps me around.
On my death the world will go broke,
for in me will have been poured its treasure,
and, desolated, the sun will stand
as empty as the wind.

74.

I want to be buried
under the angel of a tree
among the cherubim of grass
and the lion of the wind softly
in my ear and the lamb of the rain.

I am gone.
Time has happened to me,
the minute hand on the face of the earth.
Earth is a happiness of its own
as running water
as flowing grass
as the flight of birds.

75.

So many people are dead
or dying that I begin to think
it must be right;
and so many are crowding into the world
that living too must be worthwhile.

76. MIDNIGHT

As I stood heating a pan of milk on the stove
I heard my mother's voice calling me
but I remembered sleepily that she was dead
and entered my wife's room enquiring
what she wanted. Sleepily she asked
what it was I was saying and I realized
it was not my wife either whom I had heard calling.

77.

This plant could have been a person in another age, by the process that changes coal into diamonds or persons into dust. I have this to tell it, then: I can walk the street but that is not your concern or wish in the nature of things. I also enjoy my food but again it reflects nothing of your way of thinking or living. I drink water in limited amounts neither of us can live without, so we are not all that strange to each other.

Do you know that people are killing each other in streets and trains? But I am speaking of my human condition. I could withhold water from you. I could be that kind of person, and you would die, leaving me alone with my fellow men, expecting them to do no less to me, for cruelty, like most anything that lives, flourishes on what it feeds, and cruelty, like love, enjoys its own sensations.

I think it is the caring for myself that keeps me feeding water to you every day. Plant, you can't possibly die at my hands; your death would make me desperate, knowing my own life threatened, knowing that the world would end with the demise of all plants.

78. AS WE WALK OUR LIVES

I find that my life depends on a bet that I have made with a menacing character: if I pull hair out of my head three times in succession I die. The first two pulls show hair between fingers, thin, undernourished grey hair. Now I try for the third time and I'm being watched closely that I apply the same pressure against my scalp as in the first two tries. I pull. I watch as my hand comes down to the level of my eyes. I had seen a blur as I raised them hurriedly to meet my descending hand and somehow I can tell that there is a hair between my fingers, my skin sensitive to it. I look closely and there between the thumb and index finger is a hair so tiny and narrow that I do not see it except as I place it against the background of a wall. I consider myself dead, waiting for the stroke that will kill me. I am waiting, I look around me; no one is present, but who was talking to me, threatening my life? It was a voice certainly, and I begin to have a suspicion that it was me talking as usual, entertaining myself, in a manner of speaking, keeping alert to the possibilities of sudden and arbitrary unmotivated death. And now I must turn on myself and be stern. No one is threatening me, no one wants my life. I can walk the streets in safety, make distant future appointments and dine calmly at table. The world is open, as far as I wish to go. I am free and always have been.

Leave me, I tell my fear. Never return, and I order it out with a backward jab of my thumb, as though ruling out a foul play in baseball, but nothing moves. My fear does not move, and I cannot make it leave; it has no body. I cannot exorcise it; it is not evil, it is the fear of evil, and so I must live with it as company, my arm around it, its head on my shoulder.

I find that I've been hung upside down on a hook like a caught tuna or sand shark, and people are gathered around looking me over. They come and go and children push in among adult legs to get a glimpse of me. I myself am curious about this position I'm in and can't understand how it happened. I'm not about to ask the spectators who would think I'm stranger than they had realized, able to talk, still alive in this upside down position. It doesn't feel especially wrong, I'm quite comfortable. In fact, it's interesting to look at people from the bottom up, so to speak. My first view is of legs and knees pumping up and down like so many machines clomping around aimlessly and bumping into one another. I'm fascinated, and sometimes I see many legs suddenly stand still in a row like a picket fence, forming a kind of barrier, as if trying to block my view of something I would want to see or that could help me set myself right side up. But then I raise my eyes to the faces above these legs and I am distressed at what I see — stares of indifference, as if a person hanging upside down in public were a common sight, as if it even could happen to them or has happened. Young couples holding hands shrug and amble off. I watch them leave, their heads turned towards one another.

I suddenly sense being discouraged and realize too that in being discouraged it could have been me who had hung myself upside down and that is what makes the spectators so indifferent. I notice several talking about me in amused tones. Well, in that case I decide to turn right side up and with an acrobatic upward curve of my torso I leap over myself and on my feet. The crowd, astonished, begins to cheer, and some young men stroll over to ask how I had made that leap. Several girls begin to walk towards me shyly. I'm quite happy and I walk off with these young people to have a beer and to satisfy their curiosity.

80.

To look for meaning is as foolish as to find it.
What does one make of a sea shell
of such and such color and shape,
an ear or a trumpet, rose and grey?
It has been spat upon the shore
out of the sea's mouth. Is this what we mean
by our thinking? This, wondering? So
that thought itself must pause,
holding the shell lightly,
letting it go lightly.

Part IV

81. A PRAYER IN PART

Now that we have ordered well may we turn back upon suffering; after the fixed moments and precision, to seek comfort in release. Peace being with us, may we flourish in our design and discover, peaceful, that we are not human until we die; now that we have ordered all the rules may we seek out what rules us; when we have fixed all matter in a pattern, as who have emptied all problems into one and made science simple, may we break down; now that there is nothing not said or recorded and made use of may we give back the whole thing; since we are through thinking and all that is needed is to act, may we sit back; now that what remains is but to live, all means being available, may we drop them and go, go somewhere that is not calling us, that is not in us, for which we have no earthly use at all.

82.

I must make my own sun
regularly to avoid being
lost within and frozen
to death — the poem
as I make it
out of the wood
of the forest where I wander
rubbing the pieces together
picked up
as I stumble upon them.

For Robert Lowell
83.

I sit here thinking I should write,
in dread of stepping outside
the room to find nothing exists.
Here I can make something exist.
There I find myself non-existent
in doubt in empty space. Poem in hand
I can walk out of the room in safety.
I tack it upon a wall.
The emptiness gathers around it
and begins to read.

.   .   .

84.

Where is the image that will free me
of the necessity of living
by taking over the hardships?

I am asking for two lives
and I have only been able to express
the longing of this one
which is called writing the poem.

.   .   .

85.

My writing teaches me
how to die tomorrow
when the weather improves,
by dying with the sun,
a law unto itself
as I am: there is this
happiness.

86. I'M A DEPRESSED POEM

You are reading me now and thanks. I know I feel a bit
better and if you will stay with me a little longer, perhaps
take me home with you and introduce me to your friends,
I could be delighted and change my tone. I lie in a desk
drawer, hardly ever getting out to see the light and be held.
It makes me feel so futile for having given birth to myself
in anticipation. I miss a social life. I know I made myself
for that. It was the start of me.

I'm grateful that you let me talk as much as this. You prob-
ably understand, from experience; gone through something
like it yourself which may be why you hold me this long.
I've made you thoughtful and sad and now there are two
of us. I think it's fun.

I came upon the poem the way the hunter discovers the animal in the bush, with shock. I leveled my sights and was about to shoot when it spoke. "I'm here to be discovered. Place a leash around my neck and we'll travel together to your house." I lowered my weapon, amazed. The animal stepped out from its hiding and stood in front of me, waiting for me to recover. We then walked back to my house where I sprawled in my chair, unbelieving, the animal lying at my feet and looking up at me, not with adoration or servility but as an observer of another world than its own.

I thought, if I should tell others about it they would think me touched. So I decided that when they came to visit me or I them I would have this animal at my side. It might ask for food or leave to do its toilet, and all those gathered in the room would stare at it in horror, then at me, then back at the creature in disbelief, then back at me, finally to burst out, Was that speech they had heard from this animal at my feet? I'd have to nod solemnly, very much amused. Yes, speech, and the rest of the evening would go by in an uproar of excitement, delight, fear, delight, fear.

88.

Hello, drug addict, can you become a poem
   of perfect form?
Hello, Mafia, can you become a poem of
   perfect form?
Hello, schizoid person, can you become a
   poem of perfect form?
Hello, raped girl, can you become a poem
   of perfect form?
Hello, dead, napalmed man, can you become a
   poem of perfect form?
Hello, incinerated Jew, can you become a
   poem of perfect form?
If you can't, then you don't deserve to live.
You're dead, don't exist,
we want clean earth; get out, get going,
   get lost.
We have built a house for ourselves called
   the Perfect Form
and we're trying to live in it, and if you can't take
your napalmed body and your drug addicted brain
and make them into a poem of perfect form
   then you don't belong
here. Go somewhere else. Go to Vietnam where all
the imperfect bodies are and stay there and
   don't come back

[83]

to this country where only the poem of
    perfect form is wanted.
That's all we live in; you're a foreigner
    and we don't want you.
You're a kook and we hate you. You're a shit
and we wipe you off the face of the earth.
If you can't make yourself a poem of perfect form
then you have no right to be in this country.
You're here without a passport. You've lost
    your citizenship
rights. You're an alien,
    you're a spy.
You're somebody we hate.

Hello, poem of perfect form, we're home again to you
and we're going to snuggle up to you.
You give us so much comfort and pleasure.
We can run our hands over your darling self
and feel every bit of you, it's so sensuous and delicious;
it's so distracting from those bastards outside
who want to disturb us with their imperfect poems.
Fuck me, poem of perfect form.
Let me fuck you. We'll fuck each other.
We have each other, right, so let's do all the nasty
things we dream about and we'll have fun and nobody else
will know about it but you and me and me and me and me
    and you.
Wow. I don't want to hear another word
except your groans and sighs.

Finally, I'm sitting here at my desk because I'm afraid to venture into the street to be accosted by a person asking for help that would mean my whole life. I have only myself to spare and I need it to help me. Those who cry out for help have somehow lost themselves, given away or simply been robbed. I have to stay at my desk to keep myself as I am, though it's little enough, but it gives me my presence and place to be.

It is a selfish act, if I can read your thoughts, and I am ashamed, but I am fearful too to act on my impulse to love, the love for others to which I bow my head but refuse to honor because I'm afraid to love beyond myself. I know this, as my heart pounds when I get up to step outside. This is my love, I confess, and I shall remain here to write of it as my acknowledgment, to get it out for others to see and understand. They may knock on my door and ask to be let in. I may let them see me crouched over my typewriter, fearful, showing them my back, but glad that they have come to see me writing of my love, my one way to express it without losing myself in their arms.

90.

Whitman, you lost me on the open road on the way to the party at our dear Comrade's House for us all who were able to make it, wornout though we'd be, but you lost me when I wandered off the road to pick a few flowers for Him on my arrival, and stopping to wonder at their variety and beauty I sat down in their midst and began to dream that I was in His and your presence. I heard you calling me and I did call back and we went in search of each other and passed in the thick cluster of flowers, without hearing a rustle of leaves or footsteps, perhaps because both of us were listening to our fear that we were lost to each other. Your voice grew fainter to my ears as did mine to yours and soon there was silence and I was alone among the odors of the flowers. I am still here penning this message in case you decide to return for one more effort at finding me or send from our Lord's House those who miss me, thinking what a pity I am not present. This is my last hope before I expire on the ground beneath the flowers of our dear Friend.

91. EPILOGUE

The trees are tall gods
commanding a view
of my study. I bow
my head over my typewriter
and start the ceremony
of a prayer.